REFLECTIONS

OF

TODAY

INTRODUCTION

Reflections of Today are small capsules that have been presented on daily television by his author. These brief reflections that are contained in this collection have the goal to bring to your home a little faith and a lot of hope in life.

A reflection that you make is an experience that you will live on this day, and every day will serve you for a better life tomorrow. A wise man is one who takes advantage of opportunities that arise from everyday events of life.

1

HEALTHY ATTITUDES

Living with joy and happiness is an art, an art that would teach us to react healthy and wisely when encountering people, things and events.

During the course of a day I'll have half a dozen opportunities to get angry, to feel resentment, discouragement. But when that desire arises, I will react with positivity: I will not get angry and instead I will be patient- I will not be dragged by sadness, instead I will force myself to be optimistic, to laugh and to sing instead of crying.

The moment will come when I will feel the urge to hate. I will not do. I will love and understand. Simply, I will just change my primary reactions of anger, hate and sadness into healthy attitudes, and this for the simple reason that I proposed it. If you have not experimented, try this way of life. You do not need other techniques.

If you get angry, that's your choice, and if you get happy,
that's also your choice...

2

ALCOHOLISM ON THE RISE

Alcoholism is a disease, or worse a terrible enemy of Mexico and the world. Possibly more terrible than a war in the effects that it causes. Little by little is filling cemeteries with graves, and hospitals often with incurable patients. It is leaving many families with fatherless orphans. It is truly a pity and scourge filled with sadness.

How easy it is to become addicted to this vice and how difficult to disengage from it. It takes uncommon courage to do so. And don't think: the neighbor is an alcoholic, and that will never happen to me. You can be the next alcoholic, do not say no.

All for that damn first drink!

3

INFERIORITY COMPLEX

There is a very modern disease, very common and terrible called inferiority complex; let's say, the bad habit of feeling inferior to others. It is a disease that causes much harm to those suffering.

Is there way to cure it? Is there hope for these people suffering so much with this disease? There is. For example, reading the Bible, but reading it with love, hoping to find in it some words, some advice, something that inspires me, that makes me feel capable, that makes me feel like everyone else, with the possibilities of triumph .

Also, learning to pray it is a cure. But I'm not talking about prayer in desperation, that prayer without meaning, with distraction, but one that is deep in prayer, where you really ask God for aid. Me refiero a esa oración en que realmente creo en la ayuda de Dios. I'm referring to prayer that really believes in God's help. I'm referring to that prayer that really allows me to experiment what I can do, not by my strength, but with the forces from above.

Poor timid ones! So much they suffer! But they do have a remedy.

4

WHY ARE SO MANY SAD?

The world is filled with sad, hopeless and bitter people. And one asks himself: Why? Many respond: Is it possible to live differently? Is there any reason to live happy?

I just say: Do we not have a God, a loving Father who worries about us? Why do you want him? Do we not have a Mother in heaven, the Virgin of Guadalupe, who is the best mother, and that she can take care of her children? And do we not have our faith and a Church; do we not have so many good books and so many opportunities? Are there no stars in heaven?

For what do we need the days, our health? For what do we need friends, why do we need so many things that are good in the world? Why strive to keep our eyes looking toward the earth, eyes closed to such goodness, such beauty that should make us profoundly happy?

The most terrible and widespread disease is called sadness and desperation!

5

FEELINGS OF GUILT

Far more unpleasant than a toothache or stomach ache is being feeling guilty. That is, feeling remorse for having misbehaved. Sometimes they don't let you sleep; they don't let us live in peace. Does this have a solution? Is there any cure for this feeling of guilt? Certainly there is.

First thing is learning to trust God's mercy. It is true that we are sinners, and we make many mistakes, but the goodness of God is infinitely greater and deeper than all our sins.

Secondly, it is also recommended to confess frequently. Among the many recipes for living in peace, to live in tranquility, there is one that is most efficient and is also free, the one of frequent confession.

Thirdly, there is a very good remedy which consists of helping others. If you feel guilty, if you're sad, try the therapy of charity. Do not see it as something religious. Simply, do well to others, to see what happens to you.

We are guilty of many evils. What would we do without God's mercy?

6

THE WORDS WEIGH

The words you say during the day affect you for better or for worse, and the same words that someone else tells you too also do well or harm you. If, for example, many of the words that you say or hear are negative, of sadness, apathy, laziness, jealousy, hatred, out of necessity of that day must be filled with that hatred, that resentment, that sadness bearing such words.

And, if the words you say or words that others tell you are full of positive meaning, it is said that there is much joy in those words, lots of optimism, love and confidence, and very valuable, by necessity that day will be filled with joy, courage, strength and love.

If you find garbage in your garden one day, what will you do? Will you say: Oh well, leave the garbage and allow it to accumulate or pick it up and throw it away? You can't see garbage in your house, you feel bad. And why do you allow someone or yourself to throw garbage into your mind? Not a day, two, three, or four days that form towers of trash. And negative thoughts that are sad and are mental garbage, which by necessity result in a sad and dirty mind.

We must render what is bad and fill our minds with good things.

I have to repent of many inappropriate words, but not for my silence.

7

MODERN SICKNESS

A doctor said: "Many patients do not suffer from physical illness; they are sick with thoughts of sadness and discouragement. So I treat them with a recipe of good thoughts. "

I feel it is a very wise reflection from this doctor. What are those bad thoughts, the thoughts that really make people sick, even physically? Sadness: it is terrible, resentment: it is most terrible, pessimism, it is envy. All these are thoughts that get people sick, sometimes seriously sick, and sometimes affect many people.

And what are the healthy thoughts, which help us, enjoy our good health, to keep a mind, heart, and blood circulation much better? All the thoughts of love, gratitude, faith, confidence, joy, hope.

For this kind of evil one does not need to visit any doctor, because one can prescribe a remedy to himself. It involves taking that mind and emptying it as one empties a trash can or a pocket full of pots. Empty first and then attract and bring to that mind, to that pocket, good things, good thoughts, and health will automatically improve. It is relatively easy for those who want to enjoy good health.

Healthy thoughts assist our health like the best medicine

8

THE TWENTIETH CENTURY IS GONE

The twentieth century has left us, the century of lights and shadows. That was a century of indisputable technological advances. So much technological progress has been made in this century!

But, simultaneously, the century of two terrible world wars and other smaller wars that, together, are equivalent to a third world war.

The 20th century is the one in which man has made the experiment of dispensing of God just to see how he would go alone in his life. And how has it gone for him? Man is now feeling more empty and confused than ever before.

The century of the massacre of innocent lives by abortion. More innocent people have been killed by this terrible plague, than in both world wars. It was a Century that was born and has been dying in the nightmare of communism.

A century, for better or worse in which we have been chosen to live a good part of life... We enter the new century, the 21st century, with great hope, hoping not to repeat the big mistakes and major atrocities we committed in the twentieth century.

The twentieth century was a bloody century. So many wars, why?
So much blood, What was the reason?

9

ENCYCLICAL ON MORALITY

Many wonder if the rules of moral conduct are objective and valid for all times and for all people. Indeed, they are valid for all times and for all people. Also, are valid for the men of the 21st century.

That moral truth is summarized in the famous Ten Commandments of Sinai, or, even more condensed in the two commandments of the love of God and the love of thy neighbor.

At a time like ours, in which these moral truths were a little confusing, from art and grace of people who have proposed to disorient, has been very beneficial this Encyclical of Pope John Paul II entitled "Veritatis Splendor" Splendors of Truth, which in a clear, firm and modern way, are again clarifying the eternal truths of morality, those Ten Commandments, or the two that summarize everything: love God and love thy neighbor.

The moral is demanding, but clear. Immorality turns off light, intoxicates and kills.

10

THE SPIRITUAL SMOG

There has always been smog in the cities, but now the people and governments are worried. Why? Because the smog it is inhaling poison.

But how few are worried of that other spiritual and moral smog poisoning equally or worse the consciences and souls, especially the souls of the innocent! The spiritual and moral smog is that progressive deterioration of marriages. It has reached close to 30% of marriages that are breaking in a country like ours, of Christian majority.

Pornography is moral smog, which is entering softly and with good reception in the form of songs, movies and internet to our cities, our scenarios, our homes.

Also smog is violence, suicide. If we knew the actual numbers of those who commit suicide, we would really faint.

All this and much more is smog that is poisoning us all. But how many care about this moral and spiritual smog?

We like the poison and death. Our vices taste rich and our sins sweet. ¡Oh sweet sin, how rich you taste, even though you kill me!

11

BLUE SKY

There still seems to be mountains and virgin forests in Mexico, where you can breathe fresh air, where crystalline rivers flow down the mountain and where you can drink clean water. There are still some lakes that are intended to be kept up, there are meadows, there are blue seas, beautiful seas. Pero, ¡qué pena de esas ciudades donde el cielo ya no es azul desde hace mucho tiempo, y no se sabe cuándo recuperará su color! But what a pity of those cities where the sky has not been blue for a long time, and we do not know when it will regain its color!

How sad for those half-dead forests around all the big cities! How sad for those dirty rivers flowing into the sea! How sad for so many places where before you could live and now you can't!

I look for those places with light, those lakes and blue seas, the forests in which man's hand has not entered, and much less his feet. It is still possible to find those places where one exclaims: "What great pleasure, what pleasure to live in Mexico!"

How rich tasting is the water from a clear source in the mountains!

12

THE FUTURE OF YOUR CHILDREN

What will happen to your children in the coming years? Will they be the future drug addicts? Will they be the abandoned women of tomorrow? Will they be lawless men of the street? And not because those children are bad, not because you, their parents are bad, but because they will live in a terrible environment. Si el nuestro ya es malo, imagínense el que viene. If ours generation is bad, imagine the next generation.

My question is: How many are really concerned and are doing something to prevent that? Why complain, all of us; collaborate with the bad, many; collaborate with the good, few dare. There is much timidity, great ignorance. There is little energy to go heal that environment and prepare a destiny and a clean world for the children.

Who really cares? And so you ask the question, if they will not have done already: What will become of your children and your grandchildren in the coming years?

Your children are in tow a time bomb. Run for your live and who can save himself!

13

TO KNOW HOW TO READ AND WRITE

L iteracy seems to be a very obvious thing, in which it is expected that everyone is supposed to know. It is what differentiates us from an illiterate, a person who cannot read or write. However, getting straight to the point, how many really know how to read and write correctly with grammatical and syntactical correctness, without the famous spelling mistakes?

Why do we find people everywhere that trample on the grammar, syntax, and language? Many times one is concerned with the school reaching very high levels of culture. That's Fine. But you should never ignore the most important. Take care of that need first and then everything else.

I dare to ask a question. How many can read and write, even if they are wearing a suit and tie, even if they have a management position, even though they write in the press or speak on television? How many?

There are more illiterates than we think.

14

AN EXPERIMENT

We live in an era where experiments are in style. Everyone likes new activities, experiencing new sensations, discovering new things.

I would like to propose a new experiment. Try today, when you go out to the streets, even before leaving, to do a favor for someone, but do it consciously, try to find a need and try to solve it.... If you meet a poor person, give him alms; if you see a car stopped beside the road try to get close to see if they may need any assistance... Try to understand what happens to the other person. First, that person may be afraid that you've stopped to ask if he/she needed a favor. After, perhaps they will become happy, and offer you a smile and a thank you. Try to think what happens to you. You will feel at ease, you will feel happy.

Well, this is the experiment... You may want to repeat it several times during the day. It is quite possible that you will reach the conclusion that being happy is not so difficult, and the method in approach is very different from the way people usually seek happiness: wanting others to think of me, have others do favors for me and worry about me ... Being happy is exactly the opposite: to be concerned for others, to make others happy.

If you want to be happy, try to make other people happy.

15

AUTUMN IN MEXICO

After the rains, the area of Mexico resembles a garden. While traveling down the road contemplating the sides of the road filled with flowers of all colors: white, purple and yellow. The whole field is green. Autumn is possibly more beautiful than spring in Mexico.

What happened? The rains have created this miracle. It has to be said, that those who care for nature, those who allow a pine tree to grow in the forest, those who maintain a clean creek running down from the mountain, those who allow birds and flowers to live in peace, Mexico thanks you. At the same time we will criticize those that try to destroy with an ax, with their foot or with smog, the glorious nature of Mexico in autumn.

I love Mexico after rains. But I have to wait six long months to see it flourish.

16

MY HOUSE IS GETTING ORGANIZED

My home is in arrays, and it is not completed. Well worth a reflection, because it is likely that you too have done the same.

The builders were first to pass, and apart from what they had to build, they destroyed something from the house, trampled on the garden and the other floors of the house... Then came the plumbers and apart from installing the pipes and keys, they destroyed part of the masonry. Then came the carpenters, and with an attitude of being teachers and artists, they installed the doors and windows in a more or less acceptable way, but destroyed some pipes and masonry.

At last came the painters with their thick and fine brushes and painted what they were supposed to paint and what they should have not painted.

And now I find myself in need of the bricklayer, painter, electrician and plumber to return. While the glazier has failed to arrive, what do I do? Should I have the first come back and destroy the other parts? Should I call the second to return to trample the rest? When will I finish fixing my house? Has this ever happened to you?

If you fix one thing, do not break the others.

17

WHERE IS THE TRUTH?

Where is the truth? It is a question that many ask themselves. Where is the truth? Because there are thousands of opinions, thousands of religions, thousands of moral standards, and all are presented as the truth. But obviously only one can be true. How can I know? How can I discern? Does anyone have the infallibility? Is there any charisma in which I can find support and say that I'm sure, and right?

To my knowledge there is only one person, the Vicar of Christ on earth, which has that help from God to guide humanity into the true path, the authentic road.

From childhood I was taught the true path. He who was faithful to the rock of Peter had no trouble finding the truth. Today I am an adult, and I still believe in that truth, I'm continue leaning on that rock and truthfully I have not had trouble knowing where the truth is and which path I should take.

The truth of life and things exist, but not where everyone wants it to be, but where it really is.

18

GREATNESS AND MISERY

Man carries within himself his own greatness and his own misery. By this I mean that each person makes of his life and of himself what he wants.

One can climb up and reach high levels, far more than you think, and can also fall much further than you think you can fall.

This is seen more clear when a person has encountered the two experiences. When he has practically fallen to the saddest and most miserable point and felt the nausea of life. And when that man has recuperated and has slowly begun to rise and rise, and achieve a greatness that leaves us shocked.

There are many people like that. You, like all of them, have within you these two options. You can fall more than what you have fallen; but you can climb and climb to new levels with them. What will you choose for your life: the greatness or the misery? That depends on you and don't blame anyone else. You make of your life what you want.

The man carries within him a hero and a villain.
You can make either of them come out!

19

WELL SPOKEN

I read in a book that a character had made this proposal: "Do not speak ill of any man and share everything I know that is good." This sounds weird, and is something that it is unusual. Because what is fashionable today is to talk about all the worst, even if we have to invent negative things about others, and of the good and positive things according to them, to speak as little as possible. This is our reality and the saddest way to react. Behold here, a special proposal. When I see something good, I'll tell it, I'll push it into the four winds. Let's ensure that the good and positive to be told, and that positive news will cross from sea to sea, and the worst which is already known to exist, will be ignored.

If all men reacted in this manner, we would convert from good to great our land into a paradise. But what we usually do is pay attention primarily on the bad, as if there were no good. I am convinced that there are many more good things than bad, but it is the bad news that has the press, and the good must only be predicated on. It is never news when a man behaves with honor, but instead if there is a scandal, everyone has to learn of it.

I will not speak ill of any man, and of all I will say all the good that I know, "what a magnificent goal!

Do not speak of bad news, wanting something to stay.
Speak of good, although not much will stay.

20

EVERY DAY I WILL INTEND IT

Once upon a time, they asked a man who truly seemed happy, how he managed to do so. He responded in a very simple but profound manner: "Because every day I put that in my mind." And one says, "What a simple answer!" But make it profound.

Every day I intend to remove myself from all the enemies of happiness, which are the bad thoughts, thoughts of hatred, resentment, sadness, pessimism, laziness and discouragement.

And, moreover, I will work for that happiness, bringing to my life good thoughts, attitudes and deeds. I will attract thoughts that are cheerful and optimistic, love of thy neighbor, love of myself, love of life and love of all. This is the manner that this person said; I seek to be happy, because every day I put that in my mind.

There are few that are happy, because most want happiness that is free, without effort.

21

PROMISE TO BE FAITHFUL

When the bride and groom go up to the altar they make a solemn promise, so beautiful that should be written on every wall of the house. "I promise to be faithful in prosperity and in adversity, in health and sickness, and to love and honor you every day of my life."

I would underline the promise of these words: "every day". I promise not to be faithful all my life, but today, today's day, in today's health, in today's sickness, and to love you and respect you not every day, but today. And these same words that sustain that promise and support this marriage, I will repeat tomorrow, and I will repeat them the next day and every day of my life.

If this promise was fulfilled this way, how different would many marriages be that made that same great promise, but forgot about it a few days or a few months later! The promise was: For every day of this life.

One minute a day would be enough to keep a marriage afloat; a minute to ask: "how can I bring happiness to my husband or my wife today?"

22

THE SACRED FAMILY

One day in December is the feast of the Holy Family. A family formed by Joseph, Mary and baby Jesus. They were a very poor family, which had the basics to live. However, it has been the happiest family.

They were a happy family because God was there. They were a happy family because there they were praying every day. They were happy because there they worked with peace and love. There they loved life and loved each other with a great heart.

We are in dire need of that holy family to help us recover so many family values that have been taken the wind!

Oh Family of Nazareth, with just a few basic elements in life, proved to be enough to be a happy and beautiful family! We are in dire need of your intercession in our homes and in our hearts, that wonderful range of virtues of that family!

Everyone who wants to know who the most wonderful family is, should visit Nazareth and ask Joseph, Jesus and Mary how to be happy with our family.

23

31ST OF DECEMBER

O n December 31st, last day of the year, is a good time to ask ourselves a serious question: What is really left for me this year? And anticipate that question in the last moment of our lives.

What will we have at that time in our hands? Only what we have done for God and what we have done for our fellow men.

Everything else will pass, everything else is vanity, is smoke, is nothing.

If God called me today, what would I have in my hands? Everything can be resolved today, tomorrow, nothing. Today is the day of the triumphant and of the brave, tomorrow is the day of the cowards and those who do not solve things.

There is a day that has no tomorrow ... to leave things for tomorrow will probably never get done.

24

NEW YEAR

New year, you are welcomed! May all men, you in particular, feel the desire to leave behind all dead delusions, all the problems of yesterday, all the sadness and all the hatred of yesterday.

Try to restart, try to fill your life, your heart with a new enthusiasm, a joy like one of beginning. That's a new year.

Moreover, in this day we celebrate the feast of Our Lady, Mother of God. It is a gentle invitation to put in her hands this New Year. To put in her hands our hearts, our joy. We need to put all our hope that this year will truly be the best year of our existence.

We all say: Happy New Year! But there are few happy years, because men kill the roots of the tree of happiness.

25

THE DAYS PASS US BY

Every evening the day passes by and every evening time passes by. Every evening our life passes by and we feel closer to death.

What is life for many men? It's a blowout party. For others it is a beautiful mission to fulfill in this world.

Time is gold, its money, its pleasure. For others, time is a way towards eternity.

What do you choose for life? Whatever you want it. Whatever path you choose, you will have to hurry, because time passes, flies by and never returns.

Every evening our days pass us by and every evening time passes. Every evening our life passes by.

How old are you: twenty-five, forty? Rather than say that I'm twenty-five or forty years old, I should say that I'm twenty-five or forty years less.

26

HOW LIFE PASSES BY!

In these last days of the year it is good to remember the verses of Jorge Manrique in the death of his father: "Remember the sleeping soul, revive and awaken the brain, contemplating how life passes by, how death comes so quiet. How quickly does pleasure leave, then after remembering, it gives pain! "

How quickly does pleasure leave, especially if it is outside or against the law of God! How do we pass life so silent! It is needless to say. We see how the last pages of this year are falling to the ground. This year flew by. What do we have left of it and what do we have left of life?

In reality we are only left with one thing: the love that we have had for God and our neighbors.

We only have one life and we live life once. In this life many years have passed. So ... what do I think of doing with the rest of that life?

27

THE PASTORS

The birth of Jesus too had their guests, like the birth of any other child. But there the guests were very special. They weren't the most important in the world, they weren't the Pharisees. They weren't the chief priests or kings. Who were they? Some shepherds, humble shepherds who watched their flocks in the fields.

And one wonders: Why are God's tastes like this? Well, I do not know, but they are the likes of God. It was the shepherds because they were humble, simple, because they accepted the divine message, because they were docile.

And today, if you want to be one of the guests of honor, you know how: humble, simple and docile to the will of God.

God loves the humble people. Be humble, and you will enter his favorite group.

28

THE INNOCENT CHILDREN

The innocent children have their party on December 28. They are those children who died in a brutal form because of a brutal tyrant, Herod. They bothered the tyrant, which is why he killed them.

Today there are many innocent children that too bother, and therefore must be remove them from the middle. There they are, all the abandoned children, all the abused children, especially children who have no right to live. These are the new innocent.

To them and all the innocent children of the world I would like to say: "Pray to God for us, for those who have lost the innocence."

The innocent are the ones who save the world today, as the innocent Jesus. Their number is very large, because the number of Herod's is uncountable.

29

THE WISE MEN

The three wise men, Melchior, Caspar and Balthazar are the first pagans, the first Gentiles to worship the Christ child. And they brought him gifts, what superb gifts!: Gold, frankincense and myrrh. But in addition, these gifts had a very deep meaning. Gold indicated that they see him as a great king. The incense was brought as they would adore God and myrrh which they considered him a man like us.

What is our gold, our incense and our Myrrh? That is, do we consider him as a God, as a King and as a Man from his excellence?

Today gold is worshiped as a god. The incense is offered to men. Myrrh is used to embalm corpses of men.

30

SMILING DURING ADVERSITY

If you are able to face adversity with a smile, you've won.

Certainly the first response to a failure, a problem, a pain, is to get depressed, get angry and feel sad. But, try facing any one of those problems in a different manner, with a smile. You will see that emotionally you will still be at peace. You'll find that your mind is open to finding solutions.

You will see that it is different to deal with life's problems in this way. I repeat, if you are able to take adversity, all the adversities of your life with a smile, you've won.

No one hangs themselves from a tree smiling.

31

AN IDEAL IN LIFE

An ideal (standard of perfection or excellence in life) is a big, beautiful and strong method which is worth fighting for and gives meaning to life itself. A full ideal fills our existence with plenitude, enthusiasm and strength to overcome.

Today there is little talk of ideals, especially to the young. They talk about how to enjoy life, how to get a job, but how little do they talk to them about having a great ideal for life! That's why we find people everywhere devoid of substance, frustrated and disillusioned.

I think it is necessary to talk to those young people of high ideals, if we want them to be youths that are full of joy and improvement.

Behind a great ideal, there is a successful life.

32

YOU CAN

One of the things most needed by people, older people and younger people, and perhaps most urgently the oldest people, is a person to give them encouragement. Encouragement for example to study. Encouragement to you goes on loving. Encouragement to you to continue living. Because even to life, without this spirit can lose its meaning.

He who has this ability to encourage himself, and has the ability to encourage others is one of the most required benefactors at this time. Because people are very sad, and quickly lose hope. It is necessary that we must give back that faith and hope to live and to perform all activities of life.

If you want to give me something that I really need, rather than money or material things, give me encouragement and that contagious joy of living.

33

FEW PERSEVERE

To start things is a characteristic of all. We've all started something good, actually many good things in life. The pity is that many stay there, halfway, and never get things finished.

Why do few finish? It's a really small number of people that come to a conclusion, finish things and can declare victory.

The reason is very simple. At the beginning we all feel enthusiasm. We all have a burning desire to conquer that goal. But then comes the difficulties, the boredom, fatigue and there some are left. Still a few continue who have to face new challenges, new fatigues and in not seeing the tangible results we see others fall.

Who makes it to the end? Those who know how to maintain, those that have the art of giving permanent life to that enthusiasm that we felt at the beginning.

It has always been true and will remain: He who perseveres, achieves. Few dare.

34

LIVE AND SING

If as well as some artists sing and dance would live, they would be excellent models to imitate, and would have many encouraged followers. But many artists, who do fantastic roles on stage or on a court of cement or grass, after in the field of life clash badly.

What do we have to say then? I'll forgive you in how bad you live because you sing and dance? I personally prefer those artists who not only delight me with his voice, his music, but also teach me to be better. How many artists are there in this category? People who sing and dance very well on a platform and then sing and dance very well in life, are those that know how to live as true role models.

The best artist is not one who just who sings well, but he who knows how to live healthily. I like artists who know how to dance and sing, but also live.

35

THE BEST MAN WINS

If an election is won by force, that is, not by votes, the party candidate, who wins? Only that party.

If the best candidate of all is the one who wins the election, who wins? The nation wins, we all win. If the best candidate of a party, matches against the best in the Republic, who would win in this case? The nation and the political party.

Therefore, what should a good politician aspire to be? To be not only the best of his party, but be the best in the nation.

The best politician is not always the one who wins the election, but he who best serves his country.

36

BOOKS THAT INTOXICATE

Reading and food work in similar ways in us. Food serves to give strength and force to our body, and we obviously worry about what we eat. We can't afford to take in bad food because we know that it will make us more or less sick, a serious intoxication. Therefore, there is less intoxication of the stomach than of the mind.

That is, when reading something: a book, newspaper or magazine, we don't have the same caution. Everything inside, into our minds and obviously many of those readings seriously poison us. There are many more intoxicated intellectually, and with our ideas.

Tell me what you read and I'll tell how you think, how you act, or rather, who you are!

All are careful in what they eat, but very few on what they read. The result? Common intellectual intoxication.

37

HOW MUCH WOULD YOU SELL YOUR FAITH?

Things that are worth a lot are defended by teeth and nails and are not allowed to be snatched away. They defend it with everything. For example, you do not let your life be taken away because to you it is worth a lot.

How much is your faith worth. What would you be willing to give in exchange for it? We encounter even with martyrs, that is, those who have preferred to lose their life rather than lose their faith. Of these there are few nowadays, very scarce. More abound that change their faith like they change their ties.

Which ones do you look like? Actually, you can ignore what has been taken away from you, when they have taken your faith. But you can be sure that they have stolen one of greatest things you had.

If you don't defend your faith, they will take it away. And you'll lose the most important thing.

38

SOUL FOOD

I've often wondered: Why do men, when they go to a banquet, know how to enjoy eating and drinking, and instead, when they go to a church, they feel supremely bored?

Is it more important to feed the body than to feed the soul? Man is body and soul. The body is mortal, the soul never dies. So then one would expect, if I feel joy and appetite for eating and drinking well, I should feel a far greater appetite for the things of the spirit, to feed my soul.

But why do we feel hunger and thirst for material things, things of the body, and we don't feel hunger and thirst for spiritual values? Is it because our souls are very sick?

To pray is to love and be loved. If you get bored, praying, going to church, you no longer love.

39

LOVING LITTLE TO ANYONE

He who falls in love just a little with a woman or a man, will need to search for more people to fill the hole in his heart. And if they marry, the fidelity will be in constant danger. Because little love is not enough to withstand a lifetime. Instead, he who loves a man or woman with the full capacity of their heart will not need or seek other people, they will not need them. Y, si se casan, tendrán la garantía de que pueden ser fieles toda una vida. And if they marry, they will have that guarantee that they may be loyal a lifetime.

The problem of divorce is not a problem of excessive love, it's a problem of a lack of love. And faithfulness and happiness in marriage is the reward of those who have dared to love with all their hearts.

We are asked in the Bible to love God with all our heart, with all our soul, with our entire mind and with all our force. We should love our partner in a similar way.

40

THE DESIRE TO IMPROVE YOURSELF

When you no longer have the urge to improve yourself as a man or woman, as a professional, as a Christian, you have already begun to die, and die very quickly.

Life is growth, it is development. Life is identified with hope, with the illusion and desire to improve. That is, whoever possesses all these things, could say he's living. And we can say that, although he is still moving his feet, he who has been dampened and killing all hope, all desire to be better as a man, as a citizen, as a Christian, etc. is dead.

What is your situation? If you've lost all hope, you're dying, you're dying, well, and very fast. Because your soul has become wrinkled, without style, without force, and this, out of necessity has to surface in your psychology, in your body and in your organism, which will soon not resist. That is, those who have lost all hope will be the fastest to die.

The living is moving. The dead are moved.

41

LOVE AND RESPECT

The couples who love each other madly and who know how to respect each other enjoy a quality of love that is much richer and deeper than those who indulge in all kinds of experiences.

This love still exists, fortunately. The only people who believe in this richness, depth, finesse, and even romantic love are those who live it, those who do not change their love for another cheaper love.

Those who are able to love like this know how to say "I love you too much to not respect you." They are those who, later in their marriage, show class, and have the strength to love each other their whole life, that will last an entire lifetime. Because they are not only in love with a body, but they are much more with a soul.

Love knows respect. Respect is an important part of love.

42

THE TEMPLE OF NATURE

For those who suffer from chronic sadness, these words that I found in a book could help: "The Universe is the best book to study God". The vault of the sky on a starry night is the best faculty for prayer. We have heard the infinitely beautiful symphony of flowers, sunrises and sunsets that are preceded by twilight fragrant wildflowers.

For those who have faith these realities of nature give us security, a force that invite us to live with hope. But for those who have no faith; the universe, the flowers, the sunrise or God says nothing. And then, being unable to find anything beautiful in this world, I wonder: What kind of life is that?

If a flower does not impress you, it's because
many things have died in your inside.

43

GOD ALONE SUFFICES

I was impressed how a person could find amid the greatest difficulties a source of hope. It said: "This day I have been sad, I've been alone, I cry. And here I am surprised of the radiant reality that Christians live. I have God in the middle of my heart. Everything is arranged. Goodbye loneliness, goodbye sadness, goodbye tears! I have it all. God beautifies the fields and makes the birds sing. God is the worthy object of all our love. God is a friend, he's a brother. God is always faithful. "

For those who believe that in life there is no hope, no reason to suffer, no way out of a deep problem, remember these words: "God is the only one who can fill our hearts with the balm of peace and joy."

To God we can forget, reject, despise and throw out the window, but he will always remain the joy of living.

44

FEBRUARY 14

On February 14 we celebrate the day of love and friendship. Too bad this beautiful reality has been denigrated so much. Because today we call love things that are sublime and demeaning. What did you celebrate this past February 14?

We must rescue the love, that wonderful value that exists in the world. Rescue the true love in so many couples. A love that lasts, that withstands and will not break over time.

I say rescue because the pearl is mixed with the mud, selfishness with the purest love. And some stay with mud and others are left with love. Therefore, we must separate the gold from the mud, we have to purify it. For the day we lose the love, the day where there is no love on earth, we will be totally lost.

Everything depends on the fountain of that love, the heart. Nobody can give what they don't have. If the heart is clean, if the heart is pure, if the heart is healthy, the love that will be given will be a real gem, a true love. If the heart is rotten, we cannot ask him to give genuine love but pure selfishness.

Let's ask ourselves: What kind of love is in our hearts?

Where is the true love? Take me there, or I'll die.

45

EYES OF A POET

Poets have special eyes that know how to detect poetry where others see nothing.

A true artist is able to see a finished statue when he sees a piece of marble. In the same way there are some people who have eyes of faith and hope to contemplate life, and for them it transforms into an exciting adventure.

What do poets see that others don't? What does the artist see that is hidden from other people? What does the man see who has faith and hope in life and transforms it into an exciting adventure?

Once I read these words that really touched me: "The life of the soul, minute by minute, is always beautiful, precious and exciting, whatever may be the condition of the body.

I began to reflect on those words. Why was this person saying them?

That person had the eyes of a poet, artist, eyes of faith and hope, and, therefore, saw the preciousness in life, that beauty, what others cannot see, because they lack precisely that pupil, that eye that knows how to discovers art and beauty in our existence.

I want to have the quality of heart that bypasses the broken gate, and contemplates the beautiful flowers that grow beyond the fence.

46

DON'T BELIEVE ME

Do not believe me if what I say, is not true. Don't be so sure that everything you see on TV is true, because it may be a lie, and sometimes it is.

Don't believe that everything you hear on the radio corresponds to the truth. Sometimes that truth is manipulated.

Don't be so sure that everything you read in newspapers or magazines is true, because there are people who procure to tell the truth and lies together.

I advise that when you read, see or hear the media, you have a sense of self, know how to detect the truth and stay with it and also know how to discover where the lies and misinformation are, and know how to discard them.

When one says: "I read it in this newspaper, I saw it on TV, and it may be true". It may be the truth or a lie, it depends. You also have no obligation to believe what I tell you, if you're not sure that I'm telling the truth.

Among the multitude of the manipulated there are very few who manage to hold the truth. And do not believe so easily that you're not one of them.

47

WHAT DO YOU FIGHT FOR?

What are your ideals? What do you fight for in life. That is if you're fighting for something. Have you ever thought whether the ideals for which you're fighting for in your life are worthwhile or not worthwhile? Because, imagine that you spend a lifetime striving to achieve something that at the end of the day was not worth it. It's deceiving.

What are your ideals? Is it power, is it pleasure, and is it money? Ask yourself in all seriousness if that alone is worth it. Because I've met someone who said: "After a lifetime of fighting for money, I realized that money does not make us happy."

I met someone who told me: "How much would I give to have a moment of peace!" And that was a very important person.

I've found another who said, "I feel like a dirty rag." This was a person who was mired in vice.

Are your ideals transcendent? Or are they ideals that die with you in this world? What would you take to the afterlife? Why do you fight, why do you try? Why do you work?. It is important to know and be convinced why it is really worth it.

If I don't have a why and for whom to live
and fight for, my life is worthless.

48

PEACE

Whoever you are and wherever you are, is it true that you want peace, peace in Chiapas, throughout Mexico and around the world? Why? Because peace is a gift that we can't lose, and would be a luxury too expensive to lose.

By losing the peace, a thousand more things get lost: tranquility is lost, the economy suffers and panic enters. Therefore, those who dare to break the peace, should think carefully before himself and before all others, what their motives and reasons are, which must be very serious.

If each of us who want peace does a prayer, we can make an enormously long chain that will reach into heaven and we get that wonderful gift of peace.

Hopefully, this momentary disturbance of peace stays just that, a small fire which was lit in Chiapas, but a fire that will turn off in time.

Peace is a fragile and beautiful plant that grows in good hearts.

49

THE CAUSE OF THE POOR

The cause of the poor is sacred because it involves our brothers that are most in need. But we must be vigilant and pay attention in who's working for the poor. There exists a good Samaritan, who truly loves the poor, who are dying for them. Mother Teresa, for example without promotion or propaganda devoted her life, she and her nuns to make a little more pleasant the lives of thousands of the miserable. She was a Good Samaritan who hopefully will have many imitators.

But then there are others in which it is not clear if they have love for the poor, or rather, are adorned with the cause of these unfortunate, because in this way, before public opinion, they enjoy sympathy, but deep down they seek their clouded interests.

They do not seek help for the poor, they look for something else. So we must know how to distinguish between them. Not all those who speak of the poor are good Samaritans. Many put the facade of the cause of the poor or the cause of indigenous people, but to achieve other ends.

Mother Teresa of Calcutta loved the poor.
In others I'm not so sure.

52

UNTOUCHABLE THINGS

If you go out with another woman or another man who isn't your husband or your wife, you can't consider yourself a good husband or a good wife. If you betray someone, you can't say you are very good friends with her. If you leave your children to their fate, you can't consider yourself a good father. If you don't follow civil law, you could believe that you are a good citizen, but you're not.

Similarly, - and I say this because it is fashionable, if you think you're a good Christian, a good Catholic, and disobey the Vicar of Christ on earth, disobey the rules of the church, you may believe that your very Catholic, very holy, but you're not a good Christian, a good Catholic.

Again it's all about asking: What am I? There comes a time when one must self-criticize, and perhaps even conclude: "I'm not a good Catholic... I'm no longer a good citizen. I'm no longer a good father or a mother. I was that before, perhaps at another time. "But if my reality tells me otherwise, even if you publicize it to the four winds, I am no longer that.

Fidelity is one of the wonderful virtues that have left the earth. It is unusual to be a man of our word, because we no longer have our word.

53

THEOLOGICAL LIBERATION

No doubt you've heard this term more than once, "Liberation of Theology". The name sounds nice. But pay attention! What exactly does Liberation Theology mean?

Catholic theology looks for its own liberation, but what liberation, overall? Liberation from sin, liberation from enmity with God, and consequently, also the liberation of the consequences of that sin whether they be called injustice, hatred, etc.

By what means uses that good theology? It means love, dialogue, and charity.

But there is another theology, which is called the same thing, Liberation Theology, which seeks the single release of human errors and injustices, which are many. It's doesn't speak of any transcendent liberation of man. As if man only lived in this world. What means do they use? Again here, there is one big difference: hate, resentment, violence, *and guerrilla.*

Therefore, we must be able to distinguish exactly what kind of theology of liberation we mean. Because there is a good one that seeks to liberate man from his deepest evil by good means, that is for the good. But there is another part of theology that cuts a man in half and only seeks release of human things that are wrong, by means of: violence, *guerrillas*, death and hatred.

This second form truly can't be called Catholic theology.

Very often, behind a beautiful name hides a dark reality. What is the true and radical liberation of man?

54

THE MELANCHOLY

Quite a few suffer from this disease called melancholy. In a sense it is much worse than undergoing a hard time, however hard it is. Because habitual melancholy is a state of sadness, regret and disappointment, that stretches and stretches and creates a real sickness in the soul. And the worst thing is that these people believe there is no way out of it.

Well, it can have many remedies. I would like to suggest to you a fairly simple remedy, which would be: Make it a point every day to make an act of charity with your neighbor, whoever it may be. If you see that it is doing you good, increase the dose to two, three, five, until you feel good. Follow the recipe for several days, a week or ten days.

I bet you that after that time, you will not feel the same. You will begin to feel healed, you will begin to feel that life has meaning and you will start to feel love of thy neighbor, and start feeling better yourself.

The melancholy is cured with doses of love of thy neighbor: a smile, a kind gesture, charity, an advice or something that will make you think of thy neighbor and love them.

Who would have thought that loving thy neighbor as you love yourself would be the best therapy?

55

VIOLENCE

He who sows violence declares himself enemy of God which is love. He who sows violence cannot be forgiven by God until that anger and hatred stored in his heart is ripped out.

God is Love. And where God is, by necessity needs to be peace and brotherhood. God cannot be where there is hatred, when there is resentment, even in small doses.

Sometimes we complain that there is external violence, that there are weapons that fire, that there is death. Whose fault is it? The fault lays in that portion of hatred and resentment that we all store in our souls, and when put together, can have the force of an atomic bomb which could explode in any moment.

Therefore, anyone who allows bitterness, hatred and ill feelings towards his neighbor enter into his heart, is creating potency in a guerrilla or a violent man who will kill.

So before we are thinking about what happens externally, like who is firing weapons, we should ask ourselves if that same hate that the guerrilla or a man who kills is carrying, is building in our own soul. Because in a hateful heart it is very easy to pull a gun out and shoot. It is very easy, sometimes it's a matter of seconds, sometimes just a spark.

But if there is permanent peace in my heart, it will take longer to take out a gun and kill my brother.

Violence of the heart sooner or later converts into violence to kill.

56

WHAT DOES GOD WANT FROM US?

One of my favorite authors is St. Augustine. And one day while reading one of his books I found this sentence that made me abruptly stop and re-read: "Who am I, Lord, for you to ask and demand that I love you with all my heart, with all my soul and with all my strength, and you get mad if I don't do it, indeed, and you threaten me with eternal punishment? Who am I? And I began to reflect on it.

God cares for us above all one thing, nut it matters greatly. And is to love him. But not to love him in any way we want: wholeheartedly, with all your soul and with all our force.

We must conclude that unless we love, we are lost. With God we have nothing to do if we can't offer him and our neighbors a little love. But if we know how to love, we are saved. Then that love will be demonstrated in actions, with acts of love; like participating in Mass, practicing love of thy neighbor and so on.

That is why we ask ourselves: How much do I love God? How much do I love my neighbor? That is the maximum value I have. That is my salvation.

The Christian religion was very beautiful, the most marvelous one in the world, when Christians would comply with its only two commandments to love God with all your heart and love your neighbor as you love yourself.

57

LAUGHTER

L aughter is not always a sign of happiness. Not always, but it is often a simple mask of a tragedy. Why? It is because true happiness is made up of some very specific materials.

It is made of peace with God, peace with oneself and love of thy neighbor. Whoever has these materials does not need the fuss, does not need laughter. He knows, he feels and is happy.

But this happiness, this peace of heart is very threatened. Sin is there in its various forms that kill that peace. The rancor is there that is rotting the heart of man and uprooting any sign of peace. Pessimism, despair and hopelessness are there, that destroys that land, that garden that cannot grow tranquility and peace.

Do I consider myself a happy man or woman? If you are, I know why and it's no coincidence, it is because you have cultivated the flowers of happiness. You have cultivated the love of God, you've grown to love your neighbor and you have cultivated the peace of your conscience, which is why you are happy.

He who is happy does not need to prove it. He who is not, must appear. The laughter is often an appearance of happiness.

58

MOTIVATION EVERY DAY

Every day, without appointment, someone is responsible for destroying my motivations, making me tired, angry, putting me in a bad mood and thus, eroding and wasting me. Is it the one that I cross on the street; is it a problem that arrived there unexpectedly; is it that the secretary got sick and now I don't know what I have to do. Is it a payment that they are requiring me to pay before they seize and I have no money to pay. It may be that I have become ill or something happened to one of my sons. Every day there are things like this.

If I'm not well prepared, well-defended to assimilate and obligate myself to not let that peace in my soul get stolen, before noon I will be fallen, collapsed and thrown on the floor.

There is no other choice but to take a moment every day to motivate myself; to say to myself that I am more stronger than all the problems that will come today; that today nobody is going to take away that peace in my heart; that nobody will get me angry and I will not permit anyone to make me loss my serenity.

The day that I don't do it, I am lost. Without an appointment someone or something is in charge of destroying me, wearing me down and killing half of me.

Beware of those who want to rob your good mood!
Do not let them.

59

WHEN I'M 20 YEARS OLD

At the age of 14 I had a motorcycle, a noisy motorcycle that my dad bought me. When I was 16 years-old, I would go out with a group of friends and very happily would get drunk with them every week! We would also go out with a group of girlfriends, friends that were easy, very pleasant, much to our liking.

At 18 years-old, I had a very pretty and easy girlfriend. At twenty I got married out of necessity. And continued with some break-ups and some fights, and in a few years, call them happiness, bitterness, I do not know. I divorced at 25 and now I'm with another. I don't know, she says she loves me and I really like her.

How many could repeat this same story? This could be a history of falls, a history of problems, and a history that never ends, or if it does end, ends abruptly in a tragedy.

Why must life be like that? Why must start on a motorcycle? Why, then continue by car? Why carry a courtship under my own laws and not the laws of God? Why love is selfishness? Why a marriage doesn't last? Why am I carving my own failure...?

You make your own destiny. You are you happy or unhappy because you look for it.

60

SUCCESS CANNOT BE IMPROVISED

I am convinced that success cannot be improvised. It is required to pay a price, a high price.

Certainly there can be three or four who reach success by accident and improvisation. But in the same way they can also fail miserably any other day. Normally the one that is triumphant is the one who has paid a price, for example, spending hours studying. Paying the price at work, many hours of intense work. He has paid the ultimate price to not fail, I do not know how many times, but of never giving up. He has paid the price of perseverance and tenacity.

Because many who start working, as hard as it is difficult, only go halfway. It is a very high price. The one who has climbed to the summit, enjoys the rewards, looks down and remembers: How many steps I had to take? How many times I failed but did not give up? How many times did I feel like going back but I didn't? That is why success smiles at me today.

Success is across the river. You have to cross it. Triumph is found at the top. You have to climb.

61

CONVICTION

Many parents do not know what to do with their adolescents. I tried to give him a good education, where did he go to? I sent him to a college to get educated, what happened with that education?

The blame lies in that environment that has been formed, which will destroy any value, any symptom that may be good in young people. From the music they listen to, to the places of entertainment, to the ideas that surround those environments. Apart from their own passions. And it's not that these kids are bad.

But we will try a solution that I will offer you. The best way for these young people to stand firm on values is to make them defend them.

First, we must explain to them these values, for example; respect, true love, the love of study, etc. Once they have made these values their own, you must say to them, "You're going to face a world where they will want to steal all those things. You're the one that will have to fight them, the one who will have to defend them and no one else. So you know when you're in front of the TV and you desire to watch porn, you know if you see it or if you don't. You know with which friends you go with or you don't, if they are good for us or not. You know if you get on drugs or if you don't get on drugs. You know if you get drunk or if you don't get drunk. You're the one that will have to monitor, the one which must decide one way or the other. "

That is called conviction, the spirit of conviction. If you can instill this in your children, it is likely that these values will not be lost.

Convinced parents convince their children... of values.

62

CO-RESPONSIBILITY

Those who imagine that if they take their children to a college to get a good education, will solve the problems with them, make a mistake that will cost them a lot. Because at a school, however good, if anything can help, say, 25% of the educational work of the parents. The main educators are the parents of the families and they have to put that 75% of education. With their words, but especially by their testimony and their example. College just helps a little, cooperates a bit. This is a truth that we need to learn. We better learn them than to suffer the consequences later.

One finds that at college they try to give an education that is good, human, intellectual and Christian. This does not match with what they are taught at home. It does little for these children. When there is overlap between what occurs in school and what occurs in the house, then it works. So the education has that 100% of the two protagonists that collaborate: The parents of the family at 75% and the college at 25%.

If this reflection helps you, that's good! If you disagree with it, it is likely that after a few years, you will say, "How right he was!

We can help, and we will be happy to help, but we cannot replace you as a father or mother.

63

THE ART OF MOTIVATING

He who can motivate a person has achieved the ultimate in education. Because the formula for a person to do one thing is to be motivated to do so. And what does this mean? That they like it, that they have the desire to do it, that they care, that they have interest in realizing it.

Take the case of studying. When I have managed to instill my child the pleasure, the desire and have interest in studying, I have solved the problem. But while saying, reminding and repeating that they have to study while he has no desire or enthusiasm for study, I will not achieve. And this applies to the youth and applies to adults.

When I want to get my partner to do something, why do I scold him? Why do I remind him, why do I make a bad face? I will start thinking of how I can motivate, how I can make him feel like doing it, to feel illusion.

Let's go out to dinner. He has no illusion. Let's see how I can awaken his appetite, let's see how I can make him remember that beautiful place where we were. How do you make him feel like going? And then, I will not need many words. He will say: Come on. Let's go have dinner. Let's go study. Let's go to church. Let's go to work. Let's be good. Even that.

When one is motivated to be good, it costs little. But when one is discouraged, remind, scold and tell him. He won't do it.

To know how to motivate is the art of the arts; it is a magic wand that transforms people.

64

HALLELUJAH

Hallelujah is one of the most repeated words at Easter time. It is not even a Castilian word. What does it mean? It means happiness and contains everything you need to live as a Christian in the period after Easter.

Everything must be happiness; it must be a permanent hallelujah. Now, we should ask: How many of those Christians who say Hallelujah live internally a truly joyous and happy life? How many have really risen? Because resurrection means to have certainty. To have taken out the doubts of life. To have turned problems into solutions. To resurrect also means having a deep, deep joy.

How many are truly happy? How many have a soul, life, face, of happiness, of being resurrected?

To resuscitate means to get out of the grave of sorrow, of sin, of pessimism and discouragement.

Many Hallelujahs through the air. Many Hallelujahs in the churches. How much Hallelujah, how much happiness, how much resurrection there really is in the hearts of men?

The Catholic religion produces hundreds of bored people that do not take it seriously and thousands of happy people living life in plenitude.

65

YOUTHFUL MISSIONARY

I heard that during Holy Week, 2,000 youths, boys and girls, went off as missionaries. They selected 100 villages of Mexican states Michoacán, Jalisco, Coahuila and other regions. They left their vacations and were devoted to task of transmitting their faith. They were from house to house, from family to family. Trying to redo what was undone a bit. And by doing this, along with the help of pastors, many baptisms were realized. Many marriages that were broken were improved. They increased communions, confessions and mass attendance.

They were days of hard work. There were days when they barely had time to eat. There were transportation difficulties. They were towns often lost in the mountains. There were many difficulties. But in return, these young people came back with a heart full of joy and eager to return.

It's amazing how one can find the way to be happy, trying to spread that joy to others. One can increase their faith by making their faith a giant and trying to pass it to his brothers.

The best way to increase one's faith is to disseminate it. The missionaries usually don't lose faith.

66

OPERATION HELL

I would call operation hell to those bad behaviors of many people that are slowly and steadily destroying family values. You cannot call it a better name, because it really is something infernal. And, in speaking of destroying the family, I'm not talking about abstract things.

What does abortion signify, but simply to destroy a life from birth? What do premarital relations signify which are promoted and celebrated? It signifies bringing in the virus of selfishness in the sanctuary of love between a man and a woman. What does pornography signify? Trying to mistreat, crush and destroy the values of the youth.

What does the use of contraception signify, other than go against life? In this way it eats away, it goes killing and destroying the family.

And we know that, when the family is destroyed, nothing remains. All that is left is the remains of a wreck. There are no values, there is no God, there is no love; there is nothing left.

The flames of hell are hugging the family, marriage, children, and we remain committed to say that hell does not exist.

67

I HAVE AN ALMOND TREE IN MY GARDEN

I have in the center of my garden an almond tree that in the spring gets completely covered with white flowers. I like to contemplate on it, but not only that, I also like talking to that tree. And I ask it, when I'm sad, when I have problems, when it happens to me as a poet said: "There are no more flowers in my garden, they have all died," and I ask how he maintains that joy, that enthusiasm of his white flowers.

And he, in his way, responds: "My flowers are my thoughts. I procure that my thoughts be white, be good and positive. I do not let death come into me. I procure to act in a manner in which those that see me will feel a greater desire to live.

That is why, when you look at me and when you speak to me, you make me feel very happy because at least I'm helping one person. I help you think differently, to think with happiness, with enthusiasm for everything: Of life, love, problems and difficulties.

"That is why I would like to be a tree planted in the center of the hearts of all men and teach them how to live."

Blessed Almond-Tree of flower! Who could always have you blooming in the center of their heart!

68

CONTRIBUTION TO PEACE

Although you are not political, you can contribute to peace in a very rich way. How? Every time you perform an act of kindness with someone, you are contributing to peace. Every time you think well of your neighbor, every time you speak a word with goodness and every time you make an act of charity to others, you are contributing to peace.

And if everyone in the country would dedicate every day to think well of others, to speak well, to do good things, we would all be building that tree that is leafy and robust in peace.

Every time I speak ill of my neighbor, think badly of him, press a heel on him or try to hurt him, I am contributing to war and destroying the peace in my own nation. Therefore, I do not need to be a politician or be in any party. With my life, good or bad, I am collaborating and building that peace, or I am building the war and violence.

The heart is the laboratory where war or peace is prepared, as the lab is full of love or hate.

69

FORTY THOUSAND YOUTHS

Very often we think that the youth are a disaster and there is some truth there, because we see it. But not all young people are a disaster. There are great reasons for hope. For example:

The Pope John Paul II asked the Roman youth to rise and preach the Catholic faith from door to door throughout the entire city. The response was truly sobering. Forty thousand youths enlisted and organized to go preach in the old style, as it was done the first time that the Christian faith was spread. They went from door to door. They went with that youthful charisma, with such joy on their faces, newly talking of Christ, speaking of the Church, speaking of the Pope, speaking that there is a better life, when one really loves Christ.

What a response! I myself have been led to believe even more in those young people who are really a hope, as the Pope calls them, saying: "You are the hope of the Church and the hope of the world."

Believe it or not, those who will save Christianity are the youth...

70

IMPROVING THE WORLD

Whoever does not have time to be an apostolate, has no time to be Christian." This phrase, that I read one day in a book, had a great impact on me. This means that a Christian who has no time to do good to their neighbor, be in the human or spiritual order, stops, automatically, being a Christian.

However, many believe, they say, argue that they have no time, they cannot do anything, you do not have to do some kind of apostolate, that's why there are priests or perhaps someone who has no family, not have other important things to do.

However, this is for everyone, for you, for me and for anyone who wants to keep calling themselves Christian. He who does not seek or find time to convey to his brothers something that is good, whether it be their faith, an illusion for life, closeness to God, which is called being an apostolate, has no time to be a Christian.

"He who does not live to serve, do not serve to live." Those that do not help, do not worry about others, they are allied with the opposing side, that of the evildoers and of those who kill.

71

PLANTING HOPE

One of the most urgent and pressing needs of people is joy and hope. If you don't believe me, pay close attention to people's faces as you go down the street. Most people carry a straight face, a worried face, if not a bitter one. Get on a bus; look again at those faces and you'll see that most are serious and sad.

It seems so strange and unusual to find a person laughing, a person who is happy, and above all, a person with a reason to be happy.

Hence it is required urgently, even more than blood transfusions, even more than other things, people who can give and spread joy, that can give people hope. Hope in themselves, hope for the future, hope in the afterlife, hope in life.

If you have that ability to convey hope, come, we need you.

There are thousands of needs. But the greatest need is for hope. If you have hoped to spread around, come, the world needs you.

72

THE FUTURE IS BUILT TODAY

With frequency we dedicate to thinking about the future. Sometimes imagining a future of misfortune and sometimes dreaming in a wonderful future.

But in one case or another, we should think about how that future is built, where it is built. That is, how to make my future days better than that those I'm living now.

The formula is this. That happy future or that unfortunate future is built today with what we do or don't do. That is why you can guess your future. You can guess what will happen next year or the next years of your life, taking into account what you are doing today or what you're not doing today.

If u fight today, if you try today, if today you form yourself, if you dedicate yourself to build and do good things, you can be sure that your future will be good. But if you dream of a beautiful future and today you dedicate to waste time, waste money, waste your qualities, that is, to destroy the present, rest assured that your future will be very sad, very unfortunate and you will not be able to remedy it. Today our future is built whether is good or bad.

Today's day pushes tomorrow's. The day after tomorrow and the whole future. Therefore, take care of today that it be good.

73

WHEN YOU GIVE UP THE FIGHT

All of the process of corruption, individually or collectively, starts when you stop fighting, when you stop working. And it may be from discouragement, laziness or any other reason.

When one is fighting for an ideal, when one is working, that is, putting ones energy into something, even though they may fail many times, there is always the hope of victory because one doesn't get discouraged, doesn't surrender and continues fighting. And in reality the final victory is always with those who do not give up, those who are still fighting.

And this applies to the realm of holiness. Which ones make it to be saints? It isn't those who start to be saints but those who end in being saints, those who continue to fight. Which ones become great men in politics? The answer is: those who are unrelenting in battle. Which ones become great artists? The answer is: those who apart from having good qualities know how to continue to fight on improving their performance. Which ones make it to be great in any field of life? Those who are always striving to achieve.

Are you like that? Are you a permanent fighter? You must have the look and talent of a winner.

Stop fighting and you will die. Fight and strive, and you will lengthen your life. Life is movement, effort and struggle.

74

WHY ARE OTHER SECTS GROWING?

Many people ask themselves with real anxiety why so many people are leaving the Catholic faith, the faith of their grandparents, the faith of their fathers and are going to other sects or other religions of many that abound in today's market of life. They ask themselves but cannot find an answer.

In analyzing the problem, we might find many answers; but there is one in which I call the answer. The real cause is a lazy life, lived in any manner, a lukewarm Christianity, Christianity without compromise. The Christians who live this way are the candidates who are closest to going to the other side.

For them, religion doesn't signify major compromise. If they see that it goes better for them, that they feel better and have more compensation in another religion, another sect, or in anything else, they change their religion as they would a coat.

That is the problem: the Catholics who live a weak, lukewarm, mediocre Christianity, those that don't convince anyone, least of all convince the individual who lives like this. And that is the reason why any person can convince them at any time. If you live like this, get prepared to belong to another sect the day after tomorrow.

The sects grow and grow because you and I are bored and mediocre Christians.

75

DO YOU HAVE FAITH TO SHARE

Do you have faith to share, that is, do you have so much in abundance that you have spare, and therefore you can give others that faith, that vision of life and that love of God that you possess? Or is it a faith that only reaches you?

It is like when one goes shopping at the market and wants to buy many things, but when the time comes to take out the wallet, he realizes that he does not have enough, and begins to leave an object here, and then another, and then another, and takes only a few things because he didn't have enough money.

Are you like that? Are you like those that are Catholics only in moments? Maybe you're Catholic on Sunday for a moment. Maybe you're at some special event in life. But then there are hours, days and months in which it doesn't seem that you believe. It seems as if you do not have strong spiritual support. It seems that you're without a compass in life.

Today people are needed who are full, full of that faith, full of that love, full of hope to spread; because there are more poor people, more beggars for spirit than beggars for a piece of bread. There is a lot of hunger for faith, a lot of hunger for God and it is required for people who have it in abundance to share it.

When the level of faith drops in the world, the level of desperation rises. Why are there so many desperate people today?

76

CLOISTER NUNS

Many people wonder the point of having monasteries where monks or nuns live and are cloistered, dedicated primarily to prayer, to the internal work of the convent, but do not go out, do not go on roads, do not go into the world that is shouting for someone to come and help materially, spiritually or intellectually.

Apostles are needed in cities, apostles of the roads, people who go to work with others. What do they do in those convents?

And I say: Let them be, because we need someone to pray. Almost nobody does it. Let them be. Those are the people that pull God to what is needed in this world of ours. Leave them in the convents. Let them to continue praying for those who do not pray. To continue obtaining the graces of peace, brotherhood and health that are needed to walk in the bustle of work, factory and the city.

Let them continue praying in the monasteries.

John Paul II is a great benefactor of mankind above all because he is a man of God, a pioneer of prayer. His conquests and achievements are attributed to the human charisma of his personality. But he forgets that his true strength is in prayer.

Men would be invincible if we devoted less time to work on human affairs and dedicate more time to bend the knee to pray.

Prayer is boring, because we don't love. To pray is to love and be loved. True prayer only exists between those that are in love.

77

THANKS TO LIFE

There's a song that I like, in which the words begin: "Thanks to life, which has given me so much." It is an optimistic song; it is the song of the grateful, of those who know how to give thanks for life and to the one who gave us life.

It isn't the song of the pessimists, of those who complain and spend all their existence lamenting on what they haven't been given, what they are lacking or what they are suffering.

Life is an opportunity to do a thousand things. Life is to love, to think, to be happy, to make others happy, and to do wonderful things in this world. That is why, thanks be to life! despite not having it all and missing many things.

I do not complain about anything in life: which has given me so much. I am very grateful with life and I want to use all that he has given to me: The ability to think and be able to fill my life with noble thoughts and also fill the lives of others. I am grateful for the capacity to love, to love God, to love thy neighbor, to love the world, to love all people. The capacity of these hands, what these hands can do, what these hands can build in the world.

I give thanks to life, I'm not complaining. I'm not angry with life; on the contrary, I will continue to give thanks until the end.

Life is beautiful. We are the ones that destroy it,
make it ugly and kill it.

78

LOVE FOR MY COUNTRY

No one has greater love than the one who will lay down their life for someone else or something. When we find those heroes who gave their lives for their country, we have no doubt that these men and women loved their country.

Today we might ask how many of us truly feel and have in our hearts this love for our homeland. This love that is demonstrated by facts: for being a good citizen, upholding patriotic values and not just raising a flag that symbolizes the nation itself. I can feel proud, deeply proud of belonging to this nation. I can feel the heroes of my country as role models. We can feel in our own blood a genuine love, a desire to build this country, to make it better, but with deeds.

How many are there, how many are those who really love their homeland? How many are willing to give their lives for their country? Are there many?

Nobody has more love for their country than the one who will lay down his life for her. We urge politicians not to give their life but to love their country a little more.

79

OLYMPIC GAMES

Every four years we live the happiness of the Olympic Games In the world. In circumstances like this, before major tournaments, journalists are after the stars that could get a medal. And, among other questions, the one that cannot be missed is this one: Are you going to win a medal?

In the answer given there is already some impact on whether they will win or not win the medal. There are some who firmly say: I'm going to win the gold or silver. They say it with complete certainty and surety.

I think it is a mistake. It is best to be humble, it is best to say: I'll put all my effort and give the blow at the right time. Because if you say that you think you will win and make it public, you are already at a disadvantage. Certainly, we must keep a winning mentality, one has to know it and say it to himself. The coach must also know it, but nobody else. Because if not, in saying "I will win," and making it public to the four winds, will ultimately, loosen my chances, arouse the jealousy of my competitors and I will find myself often with the sad surprise that I came in fourth, fifth or worse. Therefore it is preferable not to declare victory before its time.

If you're going to win, do not say it before you do.

80

RUNNING GOD AWAY

There is a custom in our world that continues to sharpen more and more every time. And it is the custom, even more I would say the bad habit of running God away from our world. Run him away from the family, because he does us no good, because he gets in the way, because it's annoying. Run him away from society, from the cultural world, even run him away from churches. We do not want to know anything about Him.

Why? Because he gets in the way, annoys us and bothers us. Because we do not need him anymore. Moreover, there are people who presume to have achieved this great victory: We have put the man in his place. We do not need God.

But in reality what actually happens? The loser is not He. The one who loses is the man. And so, we can statistically note that where God is almost out, the man has turned against himself. There are, casually, more suicides, more selfishness, more wars and more violence.

Because in our era there have been many wars, so many disasters and so many suicides? Is it not a result of that bad habit of kicking God and running him out of our world?

I repeat that the loser is not He, because He is tranquil. He is watching us, He says: Let's see what the man can do by himself, without me. And the result is tragic. That is why, there are still some that want to say to him: Do not go, please, because then it will go very bad.

Poor man! You have run God away from your world and you're dying. Who are you going to fall back on now?

81

BE BETTER

If at any given day or any hour you realize, you get the good idea of wanting to be better and wanting to improve yourself, do not let this great opportunity pass you up. Because you understand that you don't feel the same way every day.

Usually, what is it that we feel? Longing for laziness, a desire to get carried away. But no feelings of improving. That is why, if at any minute or even a split second you get the idea in your mind of: Why not be better, why not improve myself, why not change? Do not let it go.

The change can be any day and at any time. It's about taking the first step. It's about being able to guide your own boat, and then give it continuity.

The day will come in which you have felt overjoyed in taken that first step, in making that turn to wheel. Therefore, I repeat, if you feel at any time of day a desire to change, do not let it go. Because you do not feel the same every day.

The day that someone wants to be better is a great day. Now all that's needed is to make it a reality.

82

HIDDEN STRENGTH

I am convinced that in every weak person a strong person is hidden. In every bad person there are also hidden a good person. And in an unsuccessful person, a man who feels defeated, there is also hidden a winner.

I'm not sure if you agree, but its matter of looking inside yourself, in that arsenal of forces that we all have, to seek and learn how to find that strength in the midst of my weakness. Because one thing is to be passing through a moment of weakness and another thing is to always be feeling this way. We must seize that power.

You may be passing through times of bad behavior. That is no reason for a man to be terminated, finished. There are resources and forces available, and in using them, can turn you into a good person.

Let's say the same in failure. One can reach the bottom, feel sunken and feel that there is no longer a remedy. However, there are remedies within the soul, there are forces and resources to make you succeed.

Where is the secret? It is in knowing how to find that vein of strength, that vein of kindness and that vein of resurrection. We all have a remedy and can change, while life lasts.

You're poor because you want to ... You're weak, because you want to ...I disagree. Prove it to me. I do not waste time.

83

TESTING MARRIAGE

It is not uncommon for some couples, when they decide to get married, to think and have this attitude toward their own marriage: "We'll see how it goes. We will do the test to see if we are meant for each other. If it works, we will keep going. If it fails, we will part ways.

I understand that this approach to marriage leaves an open door to failure. Before marriage they must give themselves the opportunity to see if they are really meant for each other. To get to know each other sufficiently; this would be the most important. To get to know the qualities and defects of that person and ask: "With that person as they are, with their qualities and defects, could I live with them a lifetime?"

If I'm sure, then I will make that step and get married, if I'm not sure, it is preferable not to take that step that will cause unhappiness in my life. This means that before anything you have to think, and then rethink, to see if you will decide to or decide not to do it.

But once I've decided, it is for life. Love is not for a moment. Love does not function when doubt exists if they will help, if they are going to work well. Love requires certainty. Love is for a lifetime. The stage of courtship must serve to do just that, to see if I take her or leave her. And once I take her, there is no going back, it's for a lifetime.

True love is an eternal force. Love for a while is not love.

84

FEAR OF MATERNITY

I am convinced that the greatest gift women have received is motherhood. However, today we find many women who see this gift through the prism of fear. Fear of having a child: First, because it is their first. Fear of having many, because each of them represents a new tuition, it's a new face, a new sacrifice, a new effort.

Let us recognize that in motherhood there is plenty of sacrifice, a lot of struggle. It's really a challenge for women. But it is there where she finds her greatest joy, her maximum strength where she can really become a woman.

This mentality can be seen especially in young women who are overly concerned about diets, are overly concerned about the hospital where they will go, worry too much about how many children they will have, worry about their previous problems, difficulties, etc. instead of remembering the great truth of being mothers, thanking God for bringing a child into the world, and giving value to this wonderful gift they have received.

Mother's don't like their children be afraid of them. But children also don't like their mothers to be afraid of them...

85

THE CIVILIZATION OF HAVING

The majority of men and women today consider and believe that in order to be happy you need to have many things. And they think that, if they have them, their dreams will be realized: if they have a good car, if they have a good house, a television, if they have a wonderful vacation. In always wanting we must always add more and more things.

Instead, in being deprived of one of them we assume that they will be unhappy, in which they may not be fully realized. We keep forgetting that the important thing is "being" as opposed of "having".

One thing is "to have", for example, to own all the books in a library, and another thing is "to be" wise. One thing is to have a supermarket of material things and another thing "to be" in reality happy.

I think many people are mistaken, being in pursuit of more things, more human elements, are never satisfied, always wanting more, envy those that have more than himself, and believes that when they have that refrigerator, the latest model car, when they get that position, then they will be happy. They arrive and realize that they are still not happy. Then they intend to have more.

Happiness requires less. Happiness is inside and has a lot to do with "being" and very little to do with "having".

Who could have put that into our heads that in order to be happy, we must possess many things? Someone who loves us wrong.

86

STRUCTURAL CHANGE

Karl Marx offered that the solution for Humanity was a structural change. If we change the unjust structures into healthy structures, we have found the solution. As a method to achieve this he proposed the struggle of class, the struggle of the poor against the rich, the struggle of the exploited against the exploiters, that is, create a revolution.

Jesus of Nazareth offered another completely different picture. He, instead of changing the structures, began by changing man, change, above all, the heart of the man and as a means offered something seemingly innocent and ineffectual: love. He also ignited a revolution, but not with arms, not of killing each other, but the revolution of loving one another as He has loved us.

This second revolution, when lived truthfully, produces men like Francis of Assisi, like John Paul II, like Mother Teresa of Calcutta.

When we see the representatives of this revolution of love we can come to the conclusion that this method works. In exchange, when we see the Berlin Wall fall, when we see how Russia is forced to break their barbed fences and the Cubans jumping into the sea to escape, we realize that the other revolution did not work.

Karl Marx proposed that the poor kill the rich to be happy.
Jesus did not command to kill anyone. He died to make us happy.

87

GREENHOUSE EDUCATION

We still find parents today who boast that their sons or daughters are very good. They do no evil. But, why have they achieved this? Because they have had their children in some sort of greenhouse, in an environment in which it has been virtually impossible to do evil. This is a time bomb.

I have found young people who, after leaving that fence, that familiar environment and come to face life, they have felt insecure, helpless and with a willingness to try anything bad.

I remember a girl, who had been sheltered, who even in her third year of high school, was excellent throughout. In the first three months of college, while making her own life, she became a total disaster in every area. So much that her father wanted to run her out of the house. Only three months were sufficient to demonstrate that this type of formation system does not work.

In a world like ours we must have the truth at hand. Give our children values: to want them, to love them, to defend them themselves. Train them to know how stand up for themselves in life. Say to them: This is good and this is bad, that is healthy and this is poison and you know what you do with one thing or another.

And let them go into life. They already know what is good and what is bad, they have trained and they will know how to choose. This way is much more successful than to keep trying, if it still is possible, to form your sons and daughters in a greenhouse.

Any tree can grow in a greenhouse. But the tree that grows in the steppe, that one has roots

88

TIME TO THINK

There is a quality that is priceless: the ability to think. And we don't believe that many people have this quality. It is much more common to find people who are active, dynamic people, people who do things, than this one who is always busy with a full schedule, sweating, without time to go home, even no time to rest. Work is a kind of obsession, a drug for him. They don't have time to think and they justify it, because they are not allowed; this action gets them involved more and more each day.

Fatal error. He who has no time to think, will have a hard time doing things of value in life, things of importance. All the great men, all the great directors have sought noble time, and noble time in their lives to think. Think first what you want in life. See if the goals in your existence are really valid or mediocre. See how best achieve those goals that have been proposed.

Once I found a book titled "Think and Grow Rich." It seems like a ridiculous title and yet it is a very wise title. To get rich you have to think, to be holy we must think, to be a good man we need to think, to be a good television technician we must think, to do something great in life, we must make time to think.

And the one that does not give it, will only become a disturbed executive.

If you give yourself time to think, you will improve your life, you will learn the art of getting results.

IT WILL COME ONE DAY

The day will come when you're going to be happy of all the good things you have done in your life ... The day will come when you will feel happy of all the effort you have put into forming yourself, even if it took sacrifice, effort, tenacity ... The day will come when you'll be truly proud of having done good to your neighbor, helping him, consoling him, being able to give him a hand...

And there will come a day when you feel very sad, truly deceived of the many times that you devoted to laziness ... You will feel sad because you didn't measure up; because you didn't value it, you didn't get the maximum result from the potential that you received ... You will feel very sad for the lost time in which you didn't know how to get the juice out, and maximize from the best fruit...

That day in which you will feel very happy or very sad, will be the last day of your life

- *What do you want to be in life? – They ask a teenager.*
- *What did you want to be in life? - You will ask yourself on the last day.*

90

THINK BAD AND YOU WILL NOT BE RIGHT

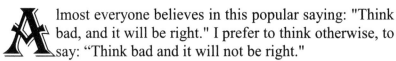

Almost everyone believes in this popular saying: "Think bad, and it will be right." I prefer to think otherwise, to say: "Think bad and it will not be right."
Perhaps those who do not think as I do are not wrong. Perhaps those who have done a favor for me have done it in good faith. Perhaps he who made me suffer did not mean any harm. Perhaps those who belong to another political party are not wrong. Perhaps those who are diverse, which are different from me are also good and are even better than me.

I prefer to say: "Think bad and you will not be right." It is preferable to be positive, to think good thoughts; one will be surprised in how you will almost always succeed. In contrast, those who carry the flag of bad thoughts, because they consider themselves to be very skillful, very clever and are always right, must recognize that they have been wrong many times.

It is true that there are bad people, but there is also good people; it is true that there is much evil, but there is also much good, even if partially hidden without propaganda and without it coming out every day in newspapers. But it is a kindness that God sees, and that is what matters.

Because most people think badly, I prefer to think well, even if I'm the only one going against the trend.

91

THEY HAVE CROSSED US OUT

Not long ago a book has come to the light that has awoken, who knows why? A lot of dust, quite controversial. It is called the Catechism of the Catholic Church. Many have had opinions even before reading it, trying to find some controversial note or a curious detail of that catechism which is quite extensive.

I would also like to have an opinion. I think that with this document they have drawn a line across it. We are already accustomed to the confusion, in that some say a truth and others say the contrary. Even among the Church leaders there were disagreements, and the people obviously did not know where to go.

Suddenly this comprehensive, clear, precise and excellent document arrives, and in my view, they drew a line across it, and when we draw a line, or we cross it out, in accepting, we stay in the same place, not accepting it and even criticizing it.

What is your attitude towards that document? Obviously we all make a decision, we all take a stance, and that is for a reason. Why do I accept it? Why do I not accept it? There is a reason why.

Am I one of the many Catholics who criticize the Catechism of the Catholic Church?

92

WHY DO I NOT ACCEPT THE CATECHISM?

L et us return to the issue of the Catechism of the Catholic Church, the book that has aroused so much controversy in many people.

The first thing to say is that if something stirs controversy in me, it is for some reason. In some way I feel attacked and I defend myself, I respond, and I also attack. Now that is fine, if I am not a Catholic,

What is the problem? That book is not for me. The book itself does not challenge me, I could read it as a book of religious culture.

If I am Catholic, and it gives me blisters, and I feel the need to attack and defend, why is it? Is it because I ignore its contents and barely know three or four badly represented topics shown through social communication, as it happens on television and through the media? Therefore what I understand from the catechism is that it is simply something like gunpowder, which can explode at any time because the ordinary ways of communicating socially have not presented a study, but have presented controversy over that book.

That's fine, but why do they attack it, why do they not accept it? It may be, perhaps, because they lived a Christianity that was very comfortable, very tranquil, which didn't require much, and now comes that catechism with the whole truth, with all the clarity, and tries to steal that Catholicism from their pocket, that way of life that is too tranquil. They have taken their peace and that is why they defend it.

The right attitude should be: I want to know the truth, even if that truth hurts. That is honesty; that is sincerity.

The Catechism is a great book. It is recommended reading, meditation and implementation.

93

A SOLD-OUT BOOK

Few dared to think that the catechism could be a bestseller. The fact is that in Spain and Mexico the first edition was sold out, and they had to print second editions of that book.

There really is some reason, there is a reason, in saying, there is interest in people to know that content, those truths of faith and we might even say that those who are against it have interest to read it, to ascertain that there were saying things that they didn't agree with to immediately go on the attack.

But to me what fills me the most, what impresses me the most is to see the town, the people had the desire, they were longing to find a beacon of light amidst so much darkness, so much uncertainty. And I think, or rather they think, they have found that beacon of light.

Incidentally, this recommendation remains open: To all those who walk in doubt, to all who want to know what to expect, to all who want to have a complete picture of the Catholic faith, this catechism gives it in a complete manner, clear and even really interesting. It is an authentic work of art.

The Catechism is one of many wonderful gifts given to us by John Paul II.

94

ENJOY LIFE

The philosophy of life that is more in vogue today is a very old philosophy, that of the Epicureans, who put it a Latin phrase "Carpe diem". It means: Seize the day, enjoy life; obviously in a selfish manner, in a manner as to squeeze juice from the existence in a manner that is less.

What happens when you follow this philosophy? There is a first time when one yearns with all their might pleasure for pleasure.

There comes a second time which consists of enjoying for a while this pleasure, which can have many forms. In reality today, one of the most developed techniques is the technique of getting the most pleasure out to life. And there's the binge, there's the drugs, there's the sex, there's everything that money, fame, etc. has to offer.

And there is a third phase: the moral hangover that is deception, not feeling satisfied with not being able to give yourself that spice of drunken pleasure. And that's why we find more and more people that are deceived, sad, unsatisfied and we will continue finding more each time, because people want to enjoy, just enjoy.

There is another way of living, another philosophy that consists of giving up our body and soul to a great ideal. What happens when we follow this other way? That great ideal at first, in the first phase scares, causing some fear, but for love can be taken seriously and followed. The second phase is precisely to experiment the difficulties, the journey, how hard it is, how difficult it is to pursue that ideal. But then comes the third phase, the phase of true importance: the result. What remains? What does that kind of life leave me? The opposite of the other: peace, happiness, personal fulfillment.

There are two philosophies, two ways of living. Everybody chooses their own.

Living for nausea...
Live to love...
Living for God and our brother...
What kind of life do I choose?

95

IF YOU DON'T DEFEND YOUR FAITH, THEY WILL TAKE IT AWAY

One of the concerns we all have is to not let people steal things from us. You look away for a moment, and you're left without a wallet, without a car and many other things. And that is why we look for alarms, we look for the police, we seek to be alert so the thief won't surprise us.

But there are thieves that enter very tranquil and are very nice, to steal something that is worth more than a car, worth more than anything else in life: my religious beliefs. And furthermore, they steal them by being tranquil, without me resisting.

I have to realize that they are robbing the most important thing because it is what gives meaning to my life, it is what gives it value, and it is what gives me strength in bitter times. That is why, the thief who makes the perfect robbery, is the one that takes away from me silently, without a problem and without resistance the faith of my parents.

This happens every day in ruthless ways. Sometimes, as a tranquilizer, they give in compensation a plate of beans, or maybe a blanket, any little thing, and I still give my thanks after they have taken away the greatest thing I had.

There are thieves in every corner. The thieves of faith are the worst, and they arrive with the face of innocent visitors who call at your door.

96

IT IS FASHIONABLE TO VISIT A PSYCHIATRIST

Today it is trendy and fashionable to go to the psychologist or psychiatrist, to cure ailments of the mind. Today people feel very sick of the soul, and obviously, believe that the ones who will heal them-sometimes they succeed, are the psychiatrists and psychologists. And so, those who want to study a well-paid career, because they will have customers, you know which one.

Why do people resort to these specialists today of the soul? The reason is simple. Because there is lack of something else. There is a lack of faith, a faith that gives light, gives strength, providing a guaranty of life, a faith in which one can be supported by.

As we live in an age where faith is lacking, that is why there is a lot of audience with the psychiatrist, with psychologists.

Am I one of those who spend their meager savings going with these people? And I have nothing against them, they ply their trade. The problem is: Where is your faith? Who took it from you? Where did you leave it? Faith cannot be replaced with psychology.

If you raise the level of faith in people, crime and despair rates would drop.

97

LOVE IS ON SALE

Love is on sale! Seize the deal! Everyone speaks of love, everyone feels like loving, everyone wants to be loved. You go see a movie, a movie about love, and soap operas about love, love that triumphs or frustrated love. Books, magazines, songs, almost everything talks about love.

But why do I say that love is for sale? Because of all its components, like if they were the petals of a flower, we have been cutting, cutting the petals until there's almost none.

They have taken everything he knows about dedication and sacrifice, which is the purest, the most rich, the essence of love. They have taken everything that signifies respect, which is another very beautiful petal of that flower. They have robbed him of hope and patience. They have taken away the worry of making the other person happy.

They have taken away so much from love that it has been left almost alone in what is sex. It is a shame that such a large truth, so beautiful, which could fill the hearts of men with life and happiness, has been left so poor by us, so poor that it can barely fill a body but not a heart.

Love is something quite different. Love is donated yourself, is to please the beloved one.

98

I WOULD NEVER DO IT

If they would tell you the truth, you would never do it. But they have always told you lie. And if you have ever done it, it is precisely because you didn't know what you were doing.

If you were told that the child you carry in your womb would be broken into pieces with a knife and then removed piece by piece ... If you were told that the child that is breathing would be poisoned by salt, trying to defend itself clinging to life, until their heart stops beating... If they would tell you the truth about what abortion is, you would never do it.

But, based on telling lies, they have achieved the most perfect murder, most terrible, most imposed, which should impact the same God which is committed frequently, calmly. The laws of some states have accepted it as if it were not a crime. But in heaven the crimes are seen for what they are. And these kids, these millions of children who could not utter a word, must speak along with God the hardest words that condemn, most terrible about humanity, about our humanity.

At the rate we're going, one day they will deliver a gold medal to the one who practices more abortions, that is, the perfect murderer.

99

YOU ARE WEAKER THAN YOU THINK

Y ou who feel so powerful ... You who feel so strong ... You who aren't afraid of anybody, you're weaker than you think.

Why do I say this? Because you have kids, and then you will have some grandchildren: beings that will be defenseless towards life. Beings that will live in a world far more corrupt than ours, a world without values, a world which may no longer have faith, a world where they will breathe like a poisonous smog pornography, materialism, hatred, revenge and the like.

You are weak because of that, you're weak, and you know it. Because any day one of your daughters, one of your sons is already a victim of drugs, and the other is a victim of alcoholism and the other had their values stolen and is mired in vice. Do you realize how weak you are?

I ask myself if you do something, if worrying about the problem, along with others trying to clean up the environment, to help values persevere, and to help your children not to die from a world that doesn't respect neither the weak nor the children. You are very weak.

Crossing your arms is a severe form of guilt.

Other works of the same author:

BOOKS IN ENGLISH:

- Shower of Roses
- The Four Seasons

BOOKS IN SPANISH:

- Lluvia de Rosas
- Matrimonios Felices
- Las Cuatro Estaciones
- Hacia las Cumbres
- La Alegría de Vivir
- Reflexiones de Hoy
- De Paso por la Vida
- Quiero Vivir
- Jesus mi Amigo

DVD'S IN SPANISH:

- Agua de Nieve
- Viaje a Tierra Santa
- Sendas de Felicidad
- Matrimonios Felices e Infelices

AUDIOS IN SPANISH:

- Las Mejores Conferencias 1

- Las Mejores Conferencias 2
- Palabras de Vida Eterna
- Las Cinco Mejores Conferencias
- Matrimonios Felices
- Familia sé tú Misma
- El Rosario, Lluvia de Rosas
- La Alegría de Vivir
- Quiero Vivir
- El Pan de Vida
- Juan Pablo II, Inolvidable
- Las Cuatro Estaciones
- Familias Felices, Familias Infelices
- La Magia del Entusiasmo
- Te he Amado Demasiado, como para no odiarte
- Lo que Nunca te han Dicho, Mujer
- Mamá, me Gusta que Seas Así
- Oraciones a la Virgen María
- Oración de San Francisco
- Himno a la Caridad
- Juventud del Alma
- La Eucaristía
- Pensamientos de Motivación I
- Pensamientos de Motivación II
- El Dulce Huésped del Alma
- Dios Mio, te Amo
- Un Día en Nazaret
- Atrévete a Creer, Esperar y Amar en grande
- Ayuno y Tentaciones de Cristo